The

Longing

That

Leads

To

Love

Jennie J. Wilkens

The Longing that Leads to Love

By Jennie J. Wilkens

Copyright © September 2025 Jennie J. Wilkens

Paperback ISBN: 979-8-9858692-2-4

EBook ISBN: 979-8-9858692-3-1

Hardcover ISBN: 979-8-9858692-4-8

Library of Congress Number: 2025914755

To request permissions, contact the publisher at jenniejwilkens@gmail.com

Edited by Kathleen McLaughlin

Cover design by @sananabeel09

Illustration concepts by Erin Markle

Illustrations by @sananabeel09

Contents

For you, the reader,

and for every person who has ever felt lost or wounded.

You are worthy of love, and you are worthy of every bit of strength you are building within yourself. Just keep going.

Unraveling

Nobody Wants the Weird Girl

So many faces and places,

dreams and dinner plates

that ultimately amounted to nothing

The strolls down the street,

the playlists on repeat

and lipstick shades I chose to keep the truth at bay

that nobody wants the weird girl

The outside is safe,

maybe even a little unique

but the inside is the tricky part that no one wants to talk about

The sinews and measures,

the pathways and pleasures,

the things that make me an apparent oddity –

a distortion of some reality –

that keeps me sleeping home alone

when all I want is a hand to hold,

and that's the catch of a life lived with less –

that nobody wants the weird girl

The loneliness becomes easy

when the lines and stories continue fleeting

and ends are made predictable

by the cycle built to continue

the pattern of promises broken into pieces,

showing me the future in all too familiar glimpses

that nobody wants the weird girl

If there's a point to all of this

I'd love to hear it,

maybe a reason for all the failed attempts

and backhanded compliments

or an explanation

for the loneliness unbreaking

in the house I tried to make a home for us both

But if it's all just late arrivals

for inconsistent smiles

THE LONGING THAT LEADS TO LOVE

I think I'll take my chances

and see this as a sign

that letting my life flow by

in a way of my own choosing

is far from the tragedy of the side that's losing

and call this all its own kind of victory

So in my curiously roaming way

I'll continue on and labor away

for what can become of pointed suffering

And in this sometimes-lonely world

I'll pay the tithe of wounds un-cured

and accept the truth

with grit and grace

that sometimes

nobody wants the weird girl

Archers

You appeared as a noble form against a backdrop of sun

and lured me in with honeyed words

and bow unstrung

I moved closer with every breath I took,

cautious but optimistic in my steps barefoot

until we were within the measured distance

of either lovers or indifference

I held my smile despite knowing your impending arrow

could be one of equal pain or love,

so eagerly hopeful it would be the latter

and I'd finally feel like I mattered

I knew the dangers of lowering my battle-wisened guard

but my signal fire heart took over to a fault,

blinding me to the selfishness in your eyes,

glinting black and bright

You drew your bow

and aimed your arrow

and I felt such joy,

having made an art of confusing the scraps of less

for a love without end,

but at the strike there was no sweet, heady rush

of the beginning of love,

but an instant spreading of poisoned hope from your arrow's hit

until all that was left

were the wounds and tears where you grabbed and twisted it

I held your eyes as you wrenched it this way and that,

silently sobbing as my bright red heart turned black

but kept my head collected

despite your remorse unaffected,

unwilling to cave under the weight of the pain

when I could just as easily treat you the same

So as you turned and fled

I pulled your arrow from my chest,

staunching the wound with my refusal to buckle and break

over a ghost who fed on deceit and shame,

and knew I could have fired it into your back,

but felt the better choice was to let you run

until the weight of clarity made you collapse

JENNIE J. WILKENS

But cowardice does serve as the best kind of fuel

for those running to avoid the truth,

and I have a feeling

you're still running today

Undying Leaves

Apollo and Daphne

You only ever wanted to be free

but both hunter and sculptor trapped you eternally –

one in the leaves of a laurel tree

and the other in the swells of marble effigy

You could have run wild and free forever

but in a plea for release you were deceived,

condemned to be the ever-rooted evergreen

in the garden of eternity

to a man you neither loved nor desired,

a villain who couldn't tell flight from a smile

As your hair and fingers turned into leaves

and your heart began to seize,

the bark clawed up from the uncaring ground,

twisting,

constricting,

round and round

like the inverted roots you didn't want to put down,

arresting your spirit nature

in a moment so heartlessly fateful,

and suddenly the sprightly nymph was no more,

and in her place

a silenced being of tragic lore

The ultimate cruelty is in the trick of it all,

to pray for escape

only to become the earthly prison

that trapped you in place,

where the love you did not hold –

that crown of undying leaves he proposed –

was thrust upon your golden head

like mortal bells

sounding

and striking

your sovereign end

Silence

I miss you,

your words, your heat,

your clever nature I learned to crave too quickly

We began so close despite the tides between us,

facing each other across the shores

with the sun and moon and stars

guiding our eyes to find

the line

between my heart and yours

It's hard to see you now,

once vivid and bright on the bank

I take one step into the unsteady waters

and then another

but I know this feeling,

the risk –

the odds already scarred on my unguarded skin

And yet I reach for you in the dark

and in the light,

morning,

night,

and all the times between the rest

but I can't feel you

and I wonder if I'm just a fool standing firm in the shadow of your words

I force the truth of my heart to die on my tongue,

wondering why I'm not enough

I try,

I fight,

knowing the sun will set all the same,

fearing I'm slowly losing who I am

in what might have been

I brave the cracking chambers in my chest

hoping East will become West,

wanting us both to give and fold,

unable to let go,

because my heart feels the pain and yet beats in defiance –

I call out for you,

I yearn,

I burn –

but all I hear is silence

Zephyr

My words were all I had to give

through the distance

and indifference

so I made them as pretty and powerful as I could –

my written heart

gifted and drifted

through the gusts of inevitable disinterest

I aligned them with the elements

to deepen their relevance,

to infuse every inked curve with meaning and desire,

that thing that ignites and takes flight

like wings in the wild

First was water

that soon fell back to the earth,

and then there was fire

that consumed,

inspired,

followed soon by the stars you never knew were there

which led me to air –

that fickle, unseen thing that evaded me

And for a time I didn't know why

but now that you're gone I see the answer,

so clear all along –

You were the air I couldn't hold on to,

that wistful, careless thing I couldn't quite have

no matter my effort,

no matter my longing

So like the wind I watched you gather

and come and go,

feeling you glide over my skin

and through my hair,

slipping through my fingers

like you were never there

Collateral Past

I feel like an exposed nerve

in an explosion stuck in slow motion

where the echoes reverberate as deeply as the pain

and I can't help but to keep reaching through the waves all the same

The world slowly bursts around me

with the shrapnel-wrapped memories

I try to filter out from the possibilities

of the luminous future my life could be,

always cutting my skin grabbing onto the wrong things

in the effort to be quick and clever

I try to mitigate the damage,

to stem the flow of the hope pouring out of me

with the tiny tourniquets of dark humor and a decently brave face

I've picked up along the way,

but the body can only take so many hits

and the heart sometimes less

before the shocks and tremors settle too deeply in

But maybe if I take that one extra step this time

I'll have made it through the shards of the past

and the fragments of distracting paths

that have led me in circles at times

And maybe if I shield my mind

instead of my heart

I can block out the debris that only serves to infuriate me,

allowing for a calmer compass

to lead me beyond the blast radius

and into the place the past can no longer reach,

that unharmed border of a life chosen for living

rather than suffering

Longing

Amare

Flutters of the heart can be dangerous things indeed,

like ripples of air carving unrelenting cracks

in the safeguards you've built against uncertainty

Such a simple little rhythm,

a tiny change in the ordinary pace of things

that can allow the warming glow to reach home

through even the thinnest of fissures,

or a deadly type of pain that slowly eats away

at your determination to risk for anything

And when you pluck that heart from the safety of its cage

and hold it out in the bright light of day

for someone else to claim,

there is no time more slowly turning

or fear more consuming

than that

Because your heart is power,

it's the bravery that is sometimes hard to find

but always there,

and offering it to another

is to relent,

to surrender,

to hope without the promise of return

But to risk the loss of power

in the name of a life intertwined with another

is a power all its own,

a force of nature to be nurtured

even with shaking hands and wearied lungs

Because the reward and the ache

spring from the same place

and there is no way to know which end the scales will tip toward,

just the comfort of the knowledge

that you would hazard heartbreak

in the quest for something more

The Lonely Field

I am walking through a field at night –

I am not lost,

having been here many times before

Some things are the same

but I see changes you've made

to the boundary of sorrow trees and wilting but dauntless flowers

The trees have sprouted more hopeful branches

reaching out past the mourning growth,

the petals a shade more vibrant when steeped in sunlight glow

I've walked this path since before it existed,

worn down by my repetitive tread

with aches and ailments in heart and head,

hoping,

healing

while searing pain into strength

to become who I was supposed to be

and thrive in vulnerability,

and offer my open-hearted desire

now having survived ice and fire

And so I wait in the twilight hour

that lies between dawn and night

where you'll cast us into darkness or light

with your words,

your actions,

how deeply you want me or don't

Where time hangs suspended seeing you down the lane,

knowing you will move toward me with the sun setting at your back

or walk away,

careless in the place I cultivated

and where I will remain

This part is pain, it's fear –

it's the daunting hoping you'll close this distance between us

and take my hand

despite what the stars and moon and sun had planned

But even when wearing this weary weight

in the tightly coiled air

my heart still thrums a hopeful beat

and my shoulders hold defiant

because I've made the place that made me

No matter your choice

or the approaching change from one state to another

there are still stars that spot the velvet sky

and blooms that decorate the earthly borders

of the place I've nurtured,

reminding me that there is beauty in the choices I've made –

that vulnerability can be a fracture-less strength –

that I remain unfolding,

unyielding,

open-hearted and ever-growing,

that it wasn't all for nothing

Longing, Loss, and Love

Loss is bitter,

love is sweet

and longing falls somewhere in between

You can feel them all at once –

a kaleidoscope that looks like hope –

because even the sweetest things

needs a measure of sorrow to fully unfold

Like the changing seasons

we try to find reason

in how a thing can start so promising

and painfully fade to nothing

The heart can be a tricky, fickle thing

that will unerringly at times defy

the laws and ways of nature

to create its own seasons and reasons

that time cannot control,

nor see nor stop or hold,

until one day the seasons have completed

or the reasons defeated,

and the heart decides it's time to find something new to inspire,

though likely not much wiser

If loss is pain

then love must be the antidote

with both in need of audacity,

of hope –

Of that vast and wild staring down of the darkness unknowing,

of taking that frightful risk of growing,

and accept that longing will always find its way

to have us reaching for what may slip away

Like seasons,

like cycles,

we risk,

we receive,

we hold fast

and sometimes fail,

but we keep steady on in spite of the storm

that is our frailty interwoven

with our humanity,

in search of that golden promise

that the balance will one day be struck

between longing,

loss,

and love

I Wish I Didn't Want It

The clawing hope casts a heavy shadow

that can sometimes suffocate

and others inebriate

at the simple idea that one day it could happen

I traded my place as a wild thing

for the lessons learned through suffering

and can tell you from both sides of the path

that neither way can last

if you're always wanting for the other

The flickering idea

of a love most sincere

kept me hanging on

long after the flame was gone,

like the promise of water in the loneliest desert

But I reached the point

when I stopped the fretting and regretting

and tried my hand at the business of forgetting,

but found that spiral-layered hope

just wouldn't let go,

like stitches curled beneath the skin

And when the ache became everlasting

I tried to trick my heart to close and refasten

but all I got was a new kind of wound –

the kind that darkly blooms in clouded solitude –

like a gnawing possibility that just won't relent,

because I still want it so badly

and I wish I didn't

Rome

The solider, the fighter,

the blade in the shadows

would wander the realm

to find what had scattered

The forger, the liar

did show his true face

for a glimpse of her smile

among pining days

The beggar, the prince,

the nomadic heart

would halt and settle

and return to the start

for a chance at the future's golden-hued day

when ichor-inked lies

could be washed away,

and set down his sword

in a dawning new world

where petals could temper

the bite of the thorns

Where wandering and longing

were left in the past,

and roses would bloom

in gardens at last

Starry-Eyed Romantic

The minutes counted,

the hours braved,

the years endured

with hearts dismayed

The time come and gone

in measures short and long

will bend the needle

of a will neither frail nor feeble,

but tired in the cycle

of the longing unchecked

in the nights without rest

But the sun will ever rise

for the starry-eyed at heart,

the moon will brightly shine

on paths traveled in the dark,

and hope will find a way to gather in the grove

at the end of the road

we all walk alone

Mourning

For My Friend

If I could tell you one more thing

it would be that I loved you

and I was sorry for your suffering

If I could ask you one more question

it wouldn't be why you did it

but what you needed

to feel like you could stay

You took your reasons with you

and we all have to move on

with the knowledge that you made your choice

in either an hour or a lifetime of pain

And although you tell me in my dreams

that you're okay

and have made peace with the choice you would change,

I hope you know that the sun will rise for you again

and when that day comes

be brave,

my sweet, sweet friend

The Thread

A golden thread formed

between my heart and yours

like a sunlit bridge I didn't expect to find

It felt vivid,

elemental,

unique in its matter

and defiant of the space and mismatched gaps between us

I thought I was strong enough to hold it together –

this brightly fragile tether –

that we could nurture and hold its glow

with our words alone,

but then your silence stretched,

speaking careless volumes

of your thoughtlessness unchecked

Despite my trying of the utmost

our thread began to fray,

little whisps breaking away

until it was a dim and thin version of what it used to be

I held strong for as long as I could,

nervous hands trying to keep it woven fast,

even warily stepping back to accommodate the slack

you caused when you loosened your grasp

I feared my efforts, my hopes

were being stained in impending sorrow

when it seemed this was a connection to uphold alone

and got my aching answer when you silently let go

In a moment of sadness

among all the threading and fretting,

the constant questioning and mending

I saw it all so simply:

For longer than I realized

I waited and ached for your words of return –

your desire to rebuild what you already had

but wanted with someone new

But that time has come and gone

like the seasons I can't control,

like the heart and connection I could not hold,

and my lack of say when you walked away

And I can now so clearly see

my fatal flaw turned into the knowledge that set me free:

That I didn't want such a vibrant and vital thing

to hit the cold hard-hearted ground,

but realized with time

I held the entirety of our thread –

that once golden, gilded bond –

and had to put it down

The Other Atlantic

I'm adrift on a ship at night
having lost count of how many days
I've been stuck in these stagnant waters
where the sun burns me,
the moon taunts me
and the stars guide me but only so maddeningly far
I hold myself tight and try to stand tall on the bow
to see if the horizon shows any signs of change
but my saltwater eyes see none,
my legs beneath me threatening to give and sway
at the next lap of water against the hull

I think I had a direction once
but my compass is broken,

my heart hazy,

my fight lazy,

and I fear this tepid dead zone may be all I ever know

If I could just turn back and chart another way

maybe the stars would shine brighter

under a different patch of sky,

leading me toward something better,

evading the lonely waves

that ceaselessly seem to beat back the current I'm trying to find

Time seems to have lost its meaning

except to remind me of its constant passing,

like the gusts of wind I try to harness

but can't keep from slipping through my forlorn fingertips

Sorrow is an unrelenting taste in my mouth

made worse by this bitter sea's brine

and for the life of me

I can't tell which shore I'm closer to –

the one I left

or the one I long to find

I keep my gaze ahead

feeling the fog of fatigue and heartbreak ever constant at my back,

unknowing how long I can hold on

now that the isolation swirls with the elements,

seemingly hellbent on capsizing the little hope I have left

My heart and brain and skin are so simply tired,

growing old out here on the sea

and I grow hateful of the plodding current

I fear I will never escape,

feeling prisoner to a fate

I tried so hard to change

And so I keep steady on,

fighting my faithlessness and the pull to dissolve into a ghostly state,

hoping the stars will soon shine through

and illuminate the way

out of this mirrored, lonely ocean,

the place I thought held the love I'd always sought,

but now wonder if it's a place in which

I'm destined to drift,

to lose,

to never cross

Seasons

The cherry blossoms weep

over an empty riverbed,

echoing my sadness

There is not a word to describe your loss

so the trees will have to do it for me

Their lives are beautiful but short,

their petals too-quickly changing

from green to pink

to dust

to ash,

but there is beauty in what doesn't last

And maybe that's the lesson

of nature's too-fast turning page –

that what we love

we only borrow for a time,

and must bravely accept the seasons

we cannot change

The Hollow Chamber

The heart is a strange and constant thing
made of four vital chambers
and countless pathways and mile marks –
the place where everything ends and starts

But there is a smaller part that sometimes overwhelms
like time overtaking our brightest memories –
the part we've all felt but cannot say
when turning it into words
becomes a wounded and weary endeavor
from which we never seem to recover

It's the space where love is supposed to grow
and maybe for a time it did

like sunlit flowers blooming in breathing ribs

but has now grown hollow and cold,

crowded out in ink and shadow

That formless echo,

the roaring repercussion

create gusts of wind,

unrelenting

The tunneling pain

and maddening pathways

can raise timeless tides of ice and flame,

cold and burning in thought and name

And yet –

It's never quite enough to finish us off –

its steadfast nature to keep beating

despite our pleas to stop,

to carry out the earthly task of creating futures beyond our past

and chart new ways forward through life's lonely lot –

to continue on in the face of loss

Leading

The Spark and the Flame

Flames can dance in darkness for a long time

until the glow of one reaches another

and they ignite,

combine

They can climb higher together,

building,

blazing,

harmonizing that fine line

between creating and consuming

But that's the risk of the tendency of flames –

the equal nature of desire and anger

and how one can quickly turn into the other

A golden hue containing the brightest blue

can gather and give

like love lulling

on coaxing winds

or shift its intention

to bitter apprehension,

leaving only burned-through ash in its path

The difference between the two extremes

is the spark of a thought

that tips the scales between wanting and not,

a constant kindling that could go either way

The feeling can change through lyric and time

with the distance measuring matchsticks or miles,

creating a love that sweetly burns through

or a violent inferno

that bleeds through brittled bone and tissue

But in the space between the spark and the flame

are the thousands of choices we make,

guiding its nature

to rage

or deliver

the kind of passion we're all striving to find,

like the delicate dance

amid those two fiery extremes

with us balancing what we do

anchored in what we choose to see

Polaris

Drifting is far too easy alone out to sea

with the air cold and faithless,

the water numbing and lulling

in the pain of becoming,

like a blanket of loneliness and confusion

It is a haunting ocean

of the not-knowing –

a place where time is a cruel ticking thing

and the stars above are pale versions of themselves,

blotted and blurred by our own mortal suffering

But I don't believe the cosmos to be so cruel

to abandon us to such a fate,

but maybe flit out of focus for a while so we'd learn

the importance of dying and reviving,

of sinking and surviving

and more importantly

the difference

In this darkened hour of the heart

we fear that bright Northern Star

has led us astray,

dimming and turning away,

but there is a way to escape this place –

to endure,

to withstand,

to hold out a little longer

against the gap between what has happened

and what we planned

The drifting has to end

and we now need to tread and try

because drowning is a quickly approaching phantom

determined to sweep us to the bottom

Our muscles will seize,

our limbs will freeze

but we must fight to ensure our future does not repeat our past,

to kick and reach and grasp

with aching eyes ever toward that wayward horizon

we feared we'd never find again

And it seems for now

it's time to be our own Northern Star

lighting down the dark

no matter the fear,

no matter the cost,

and drag ourselves through the bitter cold waters of heartache

until we arrive at that golden, promised bank

exhausted and depleted,

shaking and shivering in heavy heart-hunger

but vibrant,

vital,

and somehow never stronger

Epiphany

I believed in who you pretended to be

and still hung on when the cracks started to show

because I'm nothing if not determined

to risk heartbreak for love

But as you slowly disappeared into the cavernous eather

I realized I'd only believed in the lie,

and decided if I'd mourn someone

it would be the wounded version of myself who was too afraid to let go

So I buried her in the garden of my heart

to lay her to rest,

and by the time I was done digging

I'd forgotten your face

Surgery

I was told to keep my heart secret and cold

because only monsters would try to get close,

and love was a weakness not worth the risk,

a form of damage only the strong could predict

So I took the wounds

and cruel words

and turned the poison inward,

blaming myself for being a failure

as we all so often do

But over time I observed the joy I could not feel

and started to wonder

if those truths were even real,

and found hidden inside

the screaming desire to fight and survive

the monsters that made up the whispers in my head

and the bricked-over walls within my chest

So I dug into the pile of ever-growing ruined things

hidden within my memories

until I found an edge sharp enough to cut them out of me

but fortified with the hope that could stem the suffering,

and maybe the cynicism too

It was bloody work

and likely still not done

but over the hours turned into years

I began to feel a shift in my fear

that maybe I'd taken too much

and carved a target into my flesh instead

But if I had to perform it twice

at least I know the overzealous nicks and cuts

were worth the price

of the weightlessness I've gained

and the possibilities I've yet to claim

And in this way it was a successful procedure –

one that may have shifted my lonely future –

and spared me from a life of cowardice and withering

as the tide and time ticked idly by,

allowing me to see the shades and shapes of it all

through brand new eyes

Heart Prison

Shackles and chains

come in shades and mistakes

from the polished smiles

that hide cowardly denials

to confusing endless solitary

for a new identity

But the most insidious of all

is the prison I built around my heart

because it felt like comfort,

like armor,

like the only answer

to the hope shriveling into anger

The danger comes when the comfort and the pain

become one and the same,

as if turning away from the sun

in favor of healing left undone

will get you anywhere but cold and alone

And the mad truth of it all –

the monster I fear the most –

is that the longing might be what I'm best at,

that I've made loneliness my closest friend

and the darkest kind of vulnerability

not an enemy

but the one locked inside this cage with me

I used to scream and snarl

and rattle the rusted bars

but stopped

when presented with the self-destructive proof

that freedom was always mine to choose,

if only I'd been a little more willing to falter and lose

The fear kept me silent and still

when I saw how my honesty drove away

the weak ones who skirted the fray

and I simply didn't see how that was a blessing

And as time ticked by

within the prison I may have died

the truth slowly trickled in

past the brittle bars of my outraged heart –

the fear and misdirection

I mistook for self-reflection –

that if I created this suffocating place

I could surely destroy it too

So I set myself the task

of hacking away at it with everything I had

until the air I breathed became cleansing

and the light I saw illuminating,

revealing the key clutched in my palm all along –

that the love inside

holds the cure for all the poison of the outside world,

that a prison can become a fortress

with a simple change of focus –

and left the wounded falsehoods behind,

blending old hope and new intuition

with the second chance I'd been given,

and walked outside

Rupture/Repair

Mirrors crack,

threads fray,

tides ebb, sweeping away

Extremes flip,

pulses trip,

minds can change

and hearts can break

Time can stop

and then restart,

ticking away at day and dark

Suns will set

and moons will pale,

stars can dim, fading frail

Mirrors can set

and threads can mend,

tides can flow instead of ebb

Extremes can temper

and pulses can flutter,

minds can settle

and hearts can gather

The key is to bend instead of break,

to fix the damage with knowledge's ache

To see the sight for what it is –

a chance,

a glimpse,

maybe a gift

A splinter,

a rupture in need of repair

with thought,

with heart,

with daring and care

Alchemy

Violet the Rose

The nymph, the orphan,

the seer without sight

The virgin, the figurehead,

the girl cast aside

did bend the kingdom

with bow clutched in hand

and set it alight

with the death of a man

who thought he could rule

through lies and command

True strength she did find

and love she did too,

like blooms in the snow,

through struggle renewed

With heart and eyes open

to the malice and truths

of the lies she confronted

with the thorns that she grew,

Sweet Violet the girl

became something new –

a reckoning, a blending

of thought old and new

And when it was time

to fight and defend,

they sang

Violet the Rose,

the Queen Without End

Time

I was floating in the cosmos

in a field of purple and blue,

of pink and white,

in soft bursts of light in the blanket of black

I had no breath,

no worry,

I didn't need any;

I was simply there –

no reason,

no need,

no care

In my slow turn from one cast of stars to the next

I caught a glimpse of Time,

a pale blue ribbon

where Past, Journey, and Future met

I was confused

but knew it was the truth

and thought it strange

that Past and Future

were as close as old friends,

kept a breath apart

by the curving bend

of the Present,

but exactly where they needed to be

It was simple,

it was beautiful,

and then it was done

I had been gifted the sight

and that was enough,

because it held everything I needed –

hope,

light,

wonder,

and love

Tabula Rasa

I sought a magic potion

to help me forget him,

the touches and glances

and wounds from unearned second chances

that outweighed the knowledge I was too afraid to face

The early journey through thickets and thorns

gave me the clarity to see that I'd been harboring a score

that only served to strengthen my anger,

that poisonous thing that kept me in danger

of being eternally stuck in my suffering

But I still kept on through the forests and fields

not realizing the truth had already been revealed,

unknowingly lost in the fog of deception

and led away from the clear skies of self-reflection

in search of a fawning river that would carry me to the fountain

that would solve all of my problems,

but kept finding myself impeded by the same range of mountains

After so many failed attempts

it finally started to make sense

that my way was blocked

by the truth I did not want,

that there was no way around the mountain I was so angrily trying to move

So I banked my outrage

and accepted the pain of climbing to a higher vantage point

to find a better way to that clean-slated antidote,

gasping and tripping in the burning light of day,

having bitterly accepted that the obstacle was the only way

And in determined time

I finally gained the top of that shining summit

only to realize it was never about him,

and forgot my need for that magic potion

Dawn

I kept looking for love

in men who had none,

until I realized I'd already won

in ceasing my fear of being alone,

so I rose with the dawn

and stood on my own

My Heart is a Garden

My heart is a garden of blossoms and grass,

of present and future and past

with the gilded straw of the strength I've learned to build in myself,

a bright and ceaseless hue sprouted throughout

The bluebells are the moment of melancholy that helped me grow

that mingle with the crimson poppies of my impassioned heart in bloom

Lavender lilacs of calm silence

blend with conflicted violets

and the white-pink blossoms of my child-like delight

at simple and pretty things,

but all is never so easy and neat

when my doubts and frightful thoughts

grow choking, invading,

like insidious, jaded weeds

Gray irises show the selfishness

I try to fight against

and ivy can sometimes spread and thread

like my insecurities and anxieties unchecked,

with reminders and bruises shown in black tulips

from moments and hours of despair,

but close by are the spring green orchids

of my hopeful nature and care

for what I've rebuilt

and what I've repaired

Orange tiger lilies unfold brightly

to guard against the shadows of my past

like my faith guiding me forward and saying,

Don't look back

But I have my bad habits

like the stubborn pigweed with its deep, ruddy roots,

clinging to the truths

I sometimes hold too tight

when I'm neither wrong nor right,

but simply too afraid to let go

But newly added are the shimmering yellow bodies

of golden chrysanthemums –

the light I learned to gather from the giving sun,

reminding me to look up more often

And buried at the heart of it all

is the small but dauntless rose,

vibrantly vermilion with hope and growth,

that delicately petaled thing

protected and sometimes hindered by its own thorns

My heart is a garden of good and bad,

of light and night and all the shades and mistakes

in between

that sometimes grows wild,

sometimes serene

There are flowers of forgetting,

of anger and pain and loss,

but blooming ever brighter

are the petals of desire –

of laughter and hope and comical disaster –

of the joys and sorrows I've come to love

Sword and Shield

I picked a delicate flower from my newly mended heart

and offered it to another

while my fingers trembled

but my lungs held me together

because I knew I'd be safe no matter what

And when he declined with kind sincerity

I saw reflected back at me

the sapphire-eyed clarity

that this wouldn't be the tragedy

I'd always feared before

Because it was the first time I successfully failed

when I ached and I'd lost

but the the simple truth prevailed –

that I was still standing

and finally learning

the lesson that my angered pain

had so many times before driven away:

that I was still trying to give to someone else

what I was only just learning to give myself

And that truth was a weightlessness

that stood beside the pain,

a soothing balm that told me

I'd get the chance to try again,

and protected my newly pastel heart

from turning dark,

and finding the blessing in knowing

I wasn't just surviving but growing

And it was the purest form of oxygen

to breathe and feel the hurt

without being wounded,

to view the one standing across from me

not as a villain

but still a worthy person

who just wasn't for me

And as the wisdom of calm wove itself

through my bone and blood

I thought of all the ways old damage was being undone,

and I thanked the anxiousness

for keeping me safe up to this very moment

and then I gently told it

that it was okay to go

And I let this new kind of strength

flow through my veins

and quietly settle into my heart,

knowing I was going back to the start,

but finally with that shining sword and shield

I'd needed all along

Scripts

My life is a collection of words

inked onto pages

and read through the eather

and lived in phases

that hold color and thought,

where some lines were crossed

and some lines were not

I used to judge them all on the sides of a scale

that measured the joys

achieved or unavailed

until I saw how the strict and specific

story I was trying to compose

would never be mine if I didn't learn to let go

So I reread it forward and backward again –

the frightened script that flowed from my pen –

to find the lines and sides where I seemed to go wrong

but all I could find was the desire to belong

And the strangest thing happened when I viewed the sum total,

that the words were all simply parts of the whole,

essential –

neither good nor bad

but paced out in place

where I could reshuffle them all

and reset the stage

And that clarity granted me the perspective

that I could determine the direction

in which the rest of my life could flow,

no longer judging each word as friendly or foe

And as the author of it all

I see the lessons from the falls

no differently than all the possibilities

I can gather and arrange

into the life I now know I can change

with the ability to reframe by widening my gaze

And with this new story

from reworked future and past

I turn to the next page

and write my new path

Thank you so much for reading these poems and going on this journey with me. It is my sincere hope that you found a sense of comfort and support from them.

If you enjoyed this collection, please consider writing an honest review on Amazon and Goodreads – reviews help get books into the hands of more readers, and they're one of the best ways to support the authors and books you enjoy reading.

With love,

Jennie J.

About the author

Jennie started writing at the age of three, if you can count making pencil marks and squiggles on construction paper and then "reading" the imaginary story to her mom as writing. Diving into short stories and angsty (read: "bad") poetry as a young teen when she should have been paying attention in class, she discovered the joy of creating with words. And from that moment on, writing in one form or another became a creative joy and passionate pursuit in her daily life, though it took her well over ten years to realize she wanted to build a career around her passion for writing and storytelling.

So, a bit of a rocky start, but everyone has their journey.

A romantic to her core and inspired by the poetry of Walt Whitman, Robert Frost, and Emily Dickinson, and anyone who ever wrote or painted the beauty of landscapes, her ultimate happiness comes from the creative process of writing and sharing stories in poetic form with others. And when she's ~~procrastinating~~ not writing, she's usually watching Parks and Rec or diving into a romantasy novel with a badass heroine and dreamy love story. Or making a little sweet treat.

Jennie loves hearing from her readers. If you would like to share any thoughts or feelings about this collection, please email her at jenniejwilkens@gmail.com

.

www.ingramcontent.com/pod-product-compliance
Lightning Source LLC
Chambersburg PA
CBHW070349130626
46556CB00007B/3089